LEAKS

LEAKS

by

Susan Mrosek

Pondering Pool

ISBN 0-9762959-0-3

Edited by Sanders Editorial
520-795-4834
email: Debra@sanderseditorial.com

Published by
Pondering Pool
P. O. Box 44067
Tucson AZ 85733
520-326-4354
email: hmmm@ponderingpool.com
www.ponderingpool.com

Printed on acid-free paper
in the United States of America

THANK YOU

Eva for your vision, commitment, and support which
shot *Pondering Pool* right off the starting block and into
the laps of strangers who actually "got it." Your tremendous
generosity and creative spirit are awe inspiring.
You have my deepest gratitude.

Bill for always supporting my creativity, no matter our
situation. You skip around shedding light and lightness,
yet you're constantly deepening. You truly amaze me.
Joy Boy.

Diane for celebrating each and every one of my words
and for allowing your dear, familiar soul to permeate
my work. You are my perfect audience, my muse,
and co-conspirator.

Debbie for untangling my mind and offering me a resting place.
Your generous heart is like an unconditional home.

Toby for your keen insights and suggestions. They are
wonderfully unexpected gifts.

Debra for your delicate edits, which masterfully clarify
my voice without altering its intent, and for showering me
with your passion for words and art – keeping me elbow
deep in inspiration.

To the rest of my family – Mom, Scott, JoAnn, and Taylor –
for your repeated cheering, feedback, and stamina.

You are loved, one and all.

CONTENTS

It stands to reason.
I stand to reason.
I stand to write.
Writing helps make reason —
which is the reason I write.

TINY TALES

A pen to paper,
a thought to page, a mind to open,
a life to stage.

The Leafs

One day, Paul and Sue Leaf caught a strong wind and skipped the winding sidewalk to settle in front of my citrus grove. I was mindlessly watering the trees when they crept up behind me on the backs of 13 dancing ants. While I don't startle easily, the hose was suddenly airborne and I, Paul, and Sue were completely soaked.

Being a good sport, I invited the Leafs in for hot cocoa, dry socks, and Yahtzee. We spent the entire evening cracking jokes around the fire until half past 10, when I cranked up my leaf blower and shuttled them home.

Morning's Bud

At morning's bud she chose the day's tale. Yet before sliding out from the sheets she was already exhausted by the jubilation this day would bring. So the following dawn, she decided to let the day unfold independently. To her surprise, she awoke full of vigor, jumped out of bed, and fell flat on her face. She had no idea where to place her feet.

Nesting

Just as I round the bend I spot a leaf impaling a delightful old fellow in the forehead as he strolls the avenue. He pays no notice, but continues his trek whistling, wearing the leaf throughout the day. Night falls. The lovely man enters his bedroom suite, carefully peels the leaf from his head, and with a slight grin adds it to the others on his nightstand. Turns out he's nesting.

Beauty

As I legged my way
happily down the sunlit walk
I was consumed by beauty,
until she reached across my space
with her untamed greens,
licked my hat, and maliciously
poked me in the eye. And before
the tears could clear, she tripped me
with a rush of wild flowers stained
in such tawdry colors they
caused many an awestruck edge.
I tell you,
beauty can be painful!

Offspring

When we grow old, many, many years from now, we'll tell
our offspring (of which there are none) tales of rippled
lawn chairs that danced among kings and folded up tinier
than thimbles fit for fleas. It'll be all we can do to keep
straight faces, as the yarns spin out of control. But our
offspring (of which there are none) will enjoy beyond belief
the weave of our fabrications.

Farkel

Unfocused and frozen, I feared my mind had
moved on without me. Then I was saved.

Farkel appeared in a flash, screeching to a halt just
before slamming into my face. He looked like
a tiny boomerang, about the size of a small toenail,
with an eye on one end and a foot on the other.
It was difficult to tell whether he was coming or going.

He hovered about an inch from my nose and in
a barely audible twitter peppered the air with words
so fast I couldn't understand him. After concluding
his oration, he exploded into a fine blue mist,
and evaporated almost instantly.

Though I have no idea what Farkel said,
I'm fairly certain he is responsible for my restored
concentration and quick wit, and curiously,
my newfound love of pepper.

Sweet Bird of Paradise

Early Sunday morning, near the end of my shift,
songbirds gather outside my window to preach joy.
Their flowing black robes glisten in the sun,
freshly pressed and terribly appropriate. But wait.
Is that a touch of red I see? A tiny bird in a
hot red number makes its way toward the front,
searching for something, ruffling around almost
dance-like. It pulls out a minute shiny sliver,
clears its throat and begins.

How painfully beautiful – this sound so sweet
it candy coats the trees. Peripheral chirps completely
cease as Clara's passionate notes charge the air.

The black robed birds bow and back away,
humbled once again by the magnificent
Sweet Bird of Paradise.

Maury

The new stream was forced to gloss over one too
many stones and withdrew, arms crossed, waiting for
reciprocation. It ceased to flow. Profoundly distraught
by its own reaction, it sobbed for weeks – culminating
in a perilous torrent that screamed across the tear-stained
rocks until crashing into Maury, an enormous
pointed red leaf, whose sole purpose was to announce
the change of seasons. And so the mood passed.

The Ha

Happy to be ignored,
the Ha sat proudly on its voluptuous haunches in
the corner of my room, basking in the lack of attention.
It knew I couldn't last much longer...I was so desperate
for a laugh my brow had curdled. Then, in a surprising
burst of kindness, the Ha took pity on my sorry soul,
riled its fat ass into a frenzy, and spit a thousand
and one jokes through the air.
One was enough.

SIGNIFICANT

Untie my brain that it may be drop kicked into clarity;
fuse open my eyes that they may always see;
unclench my heart that it may absorb the incoming;
reprimand my negotiator for serving negativity over easy,
like an elegant Sunday brunch.

When Life Becomes Pointless

We're born whole. Meticulously sculpted parts,
perfectly spliced into succulent vessels, each topped
with a (very) distinct point to which we're thought to be
permanently attached. However, due to its discreet location
atop one's head, faith in its existence is often abandoned
and life becomes pointless. This may result in detachment.

In that case, with the thumb and forefinger on
either hand, employ a repetitive pinch through the
suggested space above your hair until you manage
to recapture your intent and haul it into plain view.
Here it will reignite your life's purpose,
and in turn your faith.

It will ascend into regal position automatically
once it's assured you've again gotten your point.

Now?

I would start now, but I just rose
and I'm not uncoiled yet. My legs are still
pinned at my sides, as are my wings,
and my neck lies flat against my left
shoulder. For now, the world appears
sideways, so it would be in my best interest
to wait it out...unfold naturally.
I tried to rush it once and still
haven't completely cleaned the stranded
skin from my torso. When it's time,
my limbs will pop right off
and plump out – smooth, taut, and shiny.
That's when I'll start – not now.

It

The tape stuck to her toe accruing threads, dust, nail
clippings, etc. until – laden with a week's worth of debris –
it loosened and fell off midway down the hall.
As Filbert lumbered out his doorway toward the parlor
he, without noticing, gave it another ride.

A year later, after many such forays, it had grown into a
unique, sparkling composite of their cherished lives...
often sitting with them on the veranda as they enjoyed
dessert, reminding them that every bit counts when it's
all stuck together.

Distraction

Discipline has near abandoned me. Life's ingredients
distract and distance me from my intent.
Though I'm practiced at head tilts and thrown stares,
for some reason I now lack the guide wires that
previously checked me. This is problematic,
as I'm forced to pine for help among the parish-
ioners with whose standards I invariably disagree.
The outcome will likely look quite different.

Procrastination

You see the goal posts, but decide to left-face at the
50-yard line and head toward the craggy fruit stand
beneath the bleachers for some oxygenated berries
and whipped cream. You realize you've been
distracted when the goal posts begin flagging you down
from the end zone, so you knock back the remaining
cherry red foam, dispose of the evidence, and trot off to
complete your journey down the field.
You rationalize that you could have done it differently,
but no one was looking, and you had a nasty hankering
for aerated fruit. Only now do you truly wish to attain
your goal between the posts; fortunately for you,
they've remained unconditionally receptive.

Liftoff

Our stress modules
were intended only for liftoff,
not to be
worn,
adorned,
reinforced,
or multiplied
like the
debilitating
fuselage
we've
come
to
tow.

Sanity

During the pressurized years – when she was in effect
bottled, labeled, and capped – she started a relief fund
in the name of Sanity. She collected rare humor,
kind words, large-breasted hugs, a variety of pats
on the back, and above all the wisdom to know
it would eventually pass.

Helping Hands

Don't you wonder in which corner of their bodies people
hide their support? I never see anyone walking around with
an extra hand on their shoulder or patting their back.
I, though, overflowed with so many helping hands that I
finally donated my natural born pair to the
Communal Hand Bank for the benefit of others.

High Upon the Ladder

All was well in my world. I was high upon the ladder,
and the little heads bobbing below were there to keep me
that way. I thanked them each and every day, no exceptions,
and though I occasionally lost my footing, I was never forced
down. How did I do it? It was easy – I just did.

NON SENSE

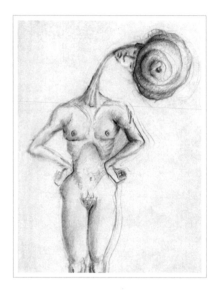

You cannot exist with a black *and* white stripe through the heart. It must be one or the other. When stripes coincide it creates nonsense; and nonsense, as we've repeatedly witnessed, is the catalyst for pumpkin's disease – the fear of orange, misshapen spheres dowsing your mind with seeds that are neither fruit bearing nor easily eradicated.

Freedom

Today the unlocking process begins – first I relocate the
lock, then I flush out the key. But will it fit? Oddly, when
much time has lapsed, the key curls into a C arc
implying "can." Now I'm able, but the key no
longer fits the lock. So I look to the Questioneer,
a job I'd love to have; all day long, only a point or nod
then "Next!" He's merely required to steer you in a
promising direction, no behind the scenes or in-depth
counseling. Hmmm, it seems I've left the key in the lock.
Never mind.

Some Other Hero

The work was done, the tile laid. We knew where to step and we didn't relish it. Not only was the gait expansive, but we were expected to sprint on our toes. I knew mine wouldn't hold up no matter the shoe, so I refused the assignment – put my foot down so to speak. And when I was ready to head home, it was gone! They'd stolen my pedal, toes and all, to accommodate some other hero with a fresh ball and heel. It's now customary for me to lag behind the group...I do enjoy the peace and quiet.

Unanimous Decision

Several heads were linked about the ears,
listening hard to each other's chatter. The outer
heads took most of the fallout, bobbing fore and rear in a
nod. This eventually lulled the center minds into
agreement, and ultimately gave birth to the
unanimous decision.

The Best Scenario

The best scenario would probably be to cocoon myself in heartfully chosen fabric and a durable red cap, then station myself beneath an old oak directly in the sun, where I can heal and root simultaneously, soaking up the energies of the critters until I, myself, grow into a squirrel.

Bird of One Feather

I'm a bird of one feather – a single feather that falls across my back, draping my spine. It's exquisitely molded about each and every vertebra then fans into a light, 3-inch fringe for good measure and looks. It even cycles the Lord's rainbow in a brilliant, colorful procession to mimic my moods. And today, I tuck it into my shorts.

Art of Expression

At rest he was 13 inches; his eyes met my knee. And he was experienced in the art of expression. He'd graffiti my calves with broad strokes of glorious color just trying to get a rise, remarking they were better than canvas – perfectly stretched and always primed. And because he was so eager to share his gift, I was honored to provide him with workspace.

Matinee

Based solely on the performance of Revor and
his son, Solmat curved the blade in half and
gave one end to me. Having missed that act, I was
unsure how to respond, but accepted. I've since
worn the blade high lest I'd puncture a toe.
One day soon I hope to catch a matinee.

Autonomy

I thought it would be all right, so I freed my arms and they
immediately left my sides to exclaim their satisfaction.
They flapped against my head, strained
my neck and displaced my glasses.
Never allow autonomy to a body part.

3-legged Avantual

The birdlike, 3-legged avantual sprouted like a weed
from my lips. So I choked back a mortified howl
and spit the mishap into the sink, where it giggled
and dove down the drain.

A Gurgle and a Stare

Vital to our planet's fair distribution of fur, the woolly bears incorporate all their clippings into fuzzy huts that sell on the open market for a gurgle and a stare. Even I can afford that.

Dairy Farm

Back here at the dairy farm, I waggle the pasture right
alongside the cows while they generously slip me
their sweet cud. I return the favor by trimming
their ears with fly paper and carnival confetti, to keep them
calm and festive. We do have fun.

HEARTWOVEN

His hand travels her flesh, careful not to upset
the delicate thread with which her skin is attached.
She fears he'll grow weary of this tension, seek someone
less fragile. But he reinstates his devotion daily,
massaging her threads with exquisite oils
to assure they'll sustain his dollface forever.

Barstofsky

No judgments please, Barstofsky.
I'm asking you politely for the last time.

You cannot continue taking advantage of my good nature
by mocking my every move with your spiked accusations
and ill-informed opinions. I'll be in shreds by day's end
and forced to seek safety under our massive Persian rug.
Actually, I'd *prefer* living beneath the expensive wool
you've ungraciously stained with your vile orations,
presumably on my behalf. It would muffle your pointed
vibrations and allow me to breathe.

Keep it to yourself, Barstofsky.
I'm no longer interested.

Indecision

Indecision hammered her bones
until they were just splinters
she hauled around in a sack of pale skin.
She carried her pain in silence.
If it weren't for the slight clatter
of bone chips as she trudged through the square,
I'd never have followed her that day
and uncovered my precious jewel,
stuck beneath the crumpled sack
at a fork in the road.

Third Eye

Give me a third eye, but not on my forehead. Position it
above my hair, so I may always look up. Then, in your best
cloudsmanship, if you would scroll the lyrics to *Lucinsky's
Look at Love* I could bow my head and project this
beautiful new perspective to life's audience.
And in the end it shall be done.

Hope in the ER

I couldn't draw her to me with my cold claw,
and prayed for the circulation of a warm hand.
Even still, I didn't know how to hold on loose
enough that she could follow, yet lead.

I told her to sit, they would come to us, she needn't hip
and toe the entire causeway to the check-in booth.
But she didn't hear me – she was already there.
And we waited.

I tossed some jokes...she didn't catch. Instead, she
dove through the bag of distractions we'd packed to
bargain with the monster, exchange pain for play.
We travel that way a lot.

Time lapsed. They insisted help was on the way.

The monster, no longer amused by her toys,
gradually resumed his preferred entertainment:
watching her spiral after the apparition he paid
to play tag down her left, no her right, yes her left side.
Suddenly she torqued through mid air toward her
vast reservoir of hope, for that is her name.

God, let it never run dry.*

Mother Ship

Life, she feels, is slipping away.
The sail on her float is full of holes,
and her uncertain spiritual direction
keeps even her compass guessing north.
She's strapped to the deck, fully racked,
skin peeled like a banana,
every nerve exposed.
She wonders how long she can
wait for the mother ship.
We wait together;
I try never to leave her side.
No one should float naked, alone.*

* These pieces are written for my sister, who somehow finds
the strength and humor to endlessly combat severe Obsessive
Compulsive Disorder. I bear witness to her daily struggle in
amazement, empathy, and prayer.

SO TO SPEAK

You pivot so eloquently around the point
no one even notices there is none.

Here nor There

Neither here nor there, just floating above myself thinking of
nothing, caring of the same, filling the air with loose
verbiage meant only to decorate the walls.

Vague Valerie

I've not the words to be clear. I'm vague Valerie,
voicing partials, lipping half words, spitting chipped
sentences. Corrections bounce off my gelatinous
structure and gather at the nape of my neck, so I
sport signs confirming this senseless condition.
And others drop coins in my cup as I search
for the proper words to allay them.

Glue

I certainly hope my disjointed yet very distinguished
thoughts, wearing their fancy words and hats,
are out there shopping for some glue.

Cocktails

Given the circuitous route in which she spoke, her
audience was unable to locate a meaning and sat
cross-eyed, with corner mouth droops and shallow
breaths, until she'd carved out a point. By then much of
the day had passed and it was time for cocktails.

Inside Out

If I keep stuffing what needs to escape,
it'll just circle my mind until gaining enough
momentum to blurt its case in public,
shoving my insides out, while my
outsides are aching to climb in.

To Dine Alone

She launched into a septic oration, dishing out blackened
ideas with her tongue onto my plate, still full from
our last meal. Oh, to dine alone.

Revelling

Words tiptoe across my lips,
slipping silently between my teeth
to revel in the coddle and curl of my tongue
and be thrust to the safe hollow of my throat.

Failed Returns

Once-spoken words rebel, attempting to reenter my mouth.
But I can't take them back, and my face is now tiled
with years of failed returns.

Originality

There came a time when all that needed saying had
been said...originality was left to those
who had not yet spoken.

CHANGE

I've grown, you see, several heads over my lifetime.
And now as I sit before the mirror with yet another one
budding, I realize it's not by chance it looks like all the
others...me. I can't handle change.

I Wore Red

I enter the bathroom and glimpse the mirror – it's me
in my blue shirt...again; the same face, the same makeshift
expression. Did I expect someone else? Perhaps I should
remove the mirror altogether. Will there ever be a
day when the colors cycle and I can honestly say,
"at last glance, I wore red."

Abduction

The abduction was clean and swift.
I never knew what took me.
I'm still awaiting my return.

Swabble, Sway, and Swoop

Underneath, we realize our lack of control and at times
accept our offbeat direction. Gladly we bend because were
we stationary, our bough could break and crack our
protective shell. This would be ugly. So we stay loose,
let it swabble and sway, even swoop.

HUNGER

I resume the right to go to bed hungry. I do not need
the "comfort" of a distended belly from the infinite food
that stocks my fridge and my mind. It's nauseating, it's
toxic...it's time to let it go. I'd be happier in moderation –
my stomach perhaps only an inch ahead of center.
Make no mistake, I will overcome the ill need to
bury myself deep within this flavorful, texture-filled habit.

Scavenger

I'm the largest scavenger fish in this pond, so bloated with
gifts I could pop. Yet I wobble along with my cavernous
mouth wide open unintentionally soliciting more.
Seems I would rather explode than to simply
shut my mug and appear ungrateful.

Obnoxious Child

I stave off my hunger until it's forced to parade
before me like an obnoxious child bent on
devouring my attention.

Temptation

Tonight perhaps I'll have the strength to defeat temptation
and zoom to bed without a final jelly cap. It's truly harmful,
you realize, to be so engorged that a waddle is your only
means of transportation and still you journey to the
refrigerator for more. Not much room left...soon I could
burst through my skin and pepper the walls.

SLUMBER

I must say I'm exhausted! I've tossed twice over and once
on my back. I've no room to lounge in this jumble of
thoughts that crowd my bed.

Angst

Her sleep was impeded as angst twisted her body,
offering no straightaways through which to stretch
her rippled legs. And it was no use trying to
adjust the headboard; her crown simply rose
to fill the newly allotted space.

Cousin Pearl

I dream in stages: first, second, and third – each
more voluptuous than the last, and always ending in
party hats with cousin Pearl.

Away Upon the Old McStream

Away upon the Old McStream a whale bellowed within
my dream. The sand was strewn for miles wide
from his desperate search for incoming tide.
When finally he stopped darkness shrouded his view,
for he was now upside down and his eyes were askew.

RIPENING

What a relief that as we age, we retain our scars on the
outside, rather than on the inner cuff.

Futility

I've taken to carefully minimizing my expressions,
attempting to retain what little elasticity remains in my face.
I smile more, hoping to smooth the pleats orbiting my
mouth, though this disturbingly enhances my crow's feet.
And I've spent hours in front of the mirror trying to design
a brow pose that could offset the frown lines.
My life is beginning to show.

The Middle

When your faculties begin discussing your future amongst
themselves, excluding you from even suggestion making,
you've reached the middle – a vast wonderland of vague
familiarities that were once unmistakably you.

Toying

As she ripened, she toyed with correcting her facial
landscape, but decided it would be a shame
to lose track of where she'd been.

FRIENDS

Hargy

I thought I was alone – and by myself this time –
just my outline beginning and ending
on the solid oak floor.

I recall feeling somewhat askew when I took my initial step.
The left end of my contour was caught on something,
perhaps a snag in the wood or a nail. It felt like someone
was standing on it, and when I craned left, sure enough
Hargy was there. He needed some company,
so I let him stay a while wrapped peacefully in my outline.

I must admit, sometimes I grow weary
of my gift – but it's rare.

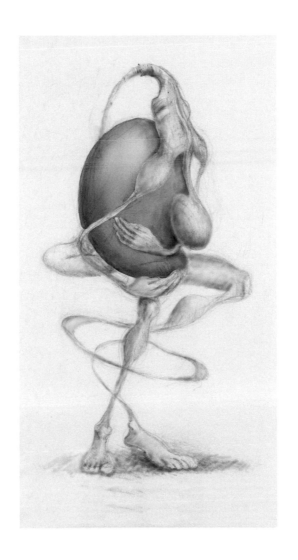

Lord Dirkson

Hamily upsets easily. She often misunderstands
Lord Dirkson's gestures, believes him to be
mocking her. In fact, he has no control
over his ticking as he's riddled with unease.
He's the kindest soul I've ever known.

Avery

Avery has a peculiar job. He verifies that anklets are
properly adorned by all the active Bettys, of which
there are exactly 10. It's not full time, yet it does keep
him busy. He sometimes daydreams about monitoring
the raucous Reggies, but overall he seems content.

Ms. Vestinbot

Translucent flesh decorates Ms. Vestinbot's 100-year-old
bones at about the same opacity as a
cheap sandwich wrap.

Aphrump and Parquay

Aphrump greets Parquay in throttle position then abruptly
sticks it in reverse. This creates a vacuum, which completely
siphons Parquay's remaining toxins and leaves him flat as a
pancake. He rolls sideways, elongates into a violin string,
and joins the others. The symphony begins.

Perrie

For breakfast, the mammoth waves of the Pacific
smashed Perrie into a flapjack, dowsed her like syrup,
and poked her into the sand like a giant fork.
Seven o'clock sharp, she was served up on shore.

Doug

A travel log is kept at Doug's
side in the event life becomes noteworthy.

Grekka

"Just passing through," were his words. He was enormous
of heart. It bulged beneath his shirt so fiercely I was forced
to stand back. They called him Grekka. But why was he
here? Why do I speak of him at this juncture?
Hell, I dunno.

Halley

About that timepiece – it was gold filigree, a tiny raised
gargoyle on the face encapsulating a beautiful blue sapphire
eye. I wore it religiously until I realized it made time run
backward and prevented me from meeting Halley for tea.

Martoosh

No one can be expected to explain the dance steps
of Martoosh as perceived by a motherless squirrel.
It just won't happen – so let's move on.

Gregory

The Greeks may have done it differently. But really, Gregory,
don't expect us to stabilize your condition without Gram's
traditional waterloo sheers. Our people have relied on them
for humph removal since the inception of grass.
Now let's extract that scowl. Just lie down and breathe
deeply, Gregory; you won't feel a thing.

Howard

It was very worthwhile, his attempt at normalcy; but
Howard was just too afield to present in a straight line.
He unraveled the heads of friends and neighbors into such
confusion they'd have to be rewound like skeins of yarn.
Howard swore one day he'd knit the most intelligent cap the
world had ever seen...but at whose expense?

Double Back Jack

Jack didn't track along a single tie. He angled in *all*
directions – no focus whatsoever. Double Back Jack
they called him; never traveled a road less than twice.
Until July 12, 1843, when he chose the north fork
and never looked back.
Had to start a whole new life though...
forgot to pack his glockenspiel.

Sufy

At home, she knitted heartfelt connections from the fuzz
that amassed between her toes and, upon entering
the village, she gathered people like moss. She was
green with hints of red, like a holiday.
Sufy – absolutely the finest lick of a being
our earth had to offer.

The Chaplets

We must applaud the Chaplets,
whose chins overlap their waists,
doubling as napkins.

SHE

She realized her head was in danger – it may be
asked to step down beside her thin, unsteady feet.
So she grabbed a hat and choked it around her hair
hoping to buy some time, but the pressure snapped
the final connection and there she stood,
with her freed head in her hat.

Security Blanket

She began as a seed like the rest of us, then hooked up
with a band of sympathetic sheep – taking root not in soil,
but in wool. Eventually she bloomed into a lovely,
old security blanket.

Hither or Ho

Not so far into the distance her look glanced back,
unrecognizable but for the demented smile and mocking
green eyes. It took her by surprise. She'd now be
unsure of anything, come hither or ho.

Worn Imagination

Within her neck lay a thin, sharp fragment from her
worn imagination, just a centimeter from intercepting
her spine. She wished it would dissolve already; she was
tired of holding still.

Beside Herself

She furrows her brow pose and fancies her hair in the
looking glass. Her dress flows beyond her slippered feet,
testing their coordination while gathering particulates
and miscellaneous debris. Juxtaposed beside herself,
adjacent to her needs (never on top of them) she often
loses sight of her surroundings.
It's no wonder she never gets anything done.

Auditioning

Her attitude was expensive.
It cost her a life where she could have belonged
without application, but was now expected to
audition her way through.

Dignity and Pride

Her ankles feigned weakness when her heels withdrew their
support, and she slid from the air onto her backside, without
spilling even a drop of dignity or a dollop of pride.

Mime

A self-proclaimed mime, she gestures wildly, scolding with
her hands the infidel seated at the back of the bus.
She's demanding full disclosure – even the private bits no
one can verify. The saints would have loved her this way.

Expectatious

She placed an inordinate amount of weight on her
expectations to flatten them into a thin, comfortable shawl.
Whether dressing up or down, she would
always be expectatious.

Near Side of Heaven

In spite of her blind devotion to sabotage her
dreams, she ended up on the near side of heaven,
parading her fine ass right up and along
the silver-lined clouds.

HE

He touched me at the inkling where I could only imagine
his feel, rather than at the knowing where it could
become oh so real.

Is That What I've Always Done?

I couldn't leave him alone.
I felt the need to occupy his space,
breathe his air so I could absorb his experience.
Is that what I've always done?

Compositionally

Compositionally,
he represents the negative space, and I
the spot of hope
in the lower right corner.

Joy Boy

He flows through my life
like positive ions weaving intricate patterns
that tickle me deep within.
Joy boy.

Armor

The sighs from his armor clatter loudly,
making me all too aware he's in need.
It comes from such depths, his dissatisfaction.
I want to crunch his armor,
get at the sweet meat inside.
But I've not the hardware to exhume him.

Lumbering Heart

He drives a hard point, gathers lilies to pad his ass,
drinks yellow ade that reeks of sunshine,
and carries a lumbering heart full of blue cheese.
He's so lovely, a moose once tried to mount him.

Treason

Lookin' for a reason, his sleep commits treason,
especially in this season, when he imagined he'd be
easin' on down the road.

At His Back Door

I peeked, he booed; we set out on the merry-go-round
again. Whenever our paths crossed, there charged venom.
But at his back door, where he hid his mansion
and all the treasures of his heart, sat a chair with my name.
Yet I was afraid to take up residence, knowing once I did,
the crown must fit or I'd surely lose the throne.

Womb of Silence

He defends against my questions by retreating into a womb
of silence where communication is forbidden and even
underwear is misunderstood.

Holes

What comes from my mind,
bores holes in his.

WE

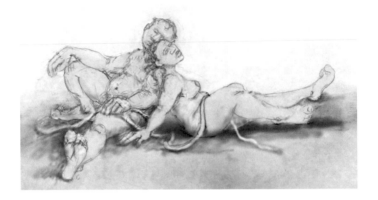

We progressed nicely into bondage, wrapped in each other's
limbs, denying all impulses to separate – and we remained as
one until dawn broke and the sun melted the plastic bands
around our buttocks and tired thighs.

Just Supposin'

Just supposin' I fed you me, one tiny spoonful at a time, and
I went down real slow and easy. And supposin' you sang
when I met your tongue, excessively and with abandon.
Then supposin' you went limp from the exhilaration of our
song, splayed yourself at the foot of our bed and laughed
uncontrollably until dawn. Just supposin'.

Beside the Point

Our legs sometimes thread across one another's laps,
and whenever possible we indulge in a
twisted neck embrace. Then all bound up,
the two of us sit beside the point,
creating exceptions to the rules.

Love Handles

Could we please slip out from betwixt these love handles
and tune our praying forks? There are people in need!

A Node and a Wire

Two individuals housing identical energy, together
become nondescript – there's nothing to note
where one ends and the other begins. And so it is
with a node and a wire that I electrify myself
on behalf of our relationship.
I'm now the portion that sizzles.

Shoe Strings

Our beliefs are separate and conflicting,
yet our souls mingle
like perfectly threaded shoe strings.

Webs

It doesn't even occur to us to dance once in a while,
we're so enmeshed in our respective webs.

Solid Hope

Later that day when the sun slept and we didn't,
the fierce nag of indecision and panic was noted missing.
I sat beside sir on the sofa and sank comfortably
into the eve like I was meant to be there.
It varied from past months in that I actually
absorbed the good will we'd set in place.
No frills (at least none were mentioned) – just solid hope.

At the Table's End

We met, we conversed, we placated and appeased.
And at the table's end we placed our heads in a pile
to choose the clearest one...mine.

WORRISOME

I strain to contain what remains.

Worry Wart

Without warning, an enormous worry wart
sprouted atop her fragile head.
It grew larger each day
until she could no longer
raise her head from her pillow.

Forced to spend countless hours in repose,
gazing at the peculiar patterns on her ceiling,
she concocted a solution
to coat the mammoth growth
and curtail its expansion.

After a brief nap,
she carefully extracted her concerns
and set them aflame.

Flesh vs. Cloth

Day 1: A full leg sits on a sofa draped in fine silk,
and it occurs to the viewer it's supposed to be
connected to something. Day 2: A little fragile, having been
poked and prodded, the leg lies flattened...becoming
one with the silk. Now we've no clue as to flesh vs. cloth.
Could this happen to us?

From Scratch

I have now entered a state of mind where there are no
indigenous life forms. I'm forced to groom my
reality from scratch.

Failsafe?
Foolproof?

Failsafe, they said. Foolproof. Where did they get their
information? I'd tried it a thousand different ways and never
got off my knees. I'm not listening to them anymore.
I'll figure it out myself.

Invasions

Let's say I trip and crash to the ground, causing a dent
where ants could congregate for town hall meetings to
plan invasions on our homes. It would not be in our
community's best interest. I cannot let that happen.
Better rethink the run.

Worry Tree

The worry tree stands proud, its spiked bark pointing
in all directions, to confuse us and draw attention away
from its black, agitated leaves. Yet its discomfort
is evident as it resists the sun and angles toward the
ground, laden with the rotted fruit it has grown to bear,
the stains from which can last a lifetime.

Refill

The fact I needed additional water was more than I could
bear. It wasn't your usual thirst; it came from the emptiness
of a hollow life – one that appeared to hold
promise and had occasionally rendezvoused with grandeur.
Still, I just couldn't ask for a refill.

Back Strap

I now require a back strap – one so stiff it forces spinal
erection, for the slump has all but folded me in half.
Oh, to enjoy a straight shot from anus to crown.

Assorted and Worn

The rubber bands were assorted and worn. Some had
lost their tension, but others constrained me to the point
of isolation. To survive, I was forced to become
malleable...I've been erratic ever since.

My Bella

She glares at me as if I've eaten her goat!
Does she expect a refund?
Bitter, disgusted Bella,
clutching her bucket of impure thoughts,
anticipating the kill, her knife dripping
with the love she carved from Eggert's heart.

Ah, my Bella, what can I say?

Cunning and crisp, she misdirects
a skirmish toward the electrified fence
hoping to insight pain and suffering.

My sick, twisted Bella.
She treats me like a mad child's toy.

Enough my Bella, enough.

Disengaged

Now and then, here and there, I stop short of
tomorrow to focus on today. But with all my
affiliated strings tangled in my crown of thorns,
I crumble like a freed marionette suddenly
realizing it's been disengaged.

The Bulge

My sides are beginning to extend beyond my waistband,
interfering with my elbow as it attempts to relax at
my side. I can feel the bulge. Or is it that I've been
training my arm at a different angle and in fact nothing
has changed? Hmmm.

Stiffened Silk

You look on lovingly; I look away. I can't take the notice.
I'm afraid to be seen the way I am, without my beautiful
cloth. My silk has stiffened, stabbing my skin, leaving
reddened marks to match my crying eyes.

Reality Op

I judge it all, nothing jets past my scrutiny. The filters are
always at full grind. What if something tawdry slips
through? It could buckle the whole system, and we're so
close to finishing our reality op.

Heir

I'm heir to a castle packed with the most stringent
disciplinary tools one could imagine.
Dragged about the dungeon floor for centuries, these
tools have become razor sharp – dangerously
proficient at slicing the "good life" in two.

Faces

I can't tell if I've always made these faces,
or if they're just now answering back.

HERE AND THERE

I'm reasonably sure
I've ingested a powerchub bug.
I feel a motor purring inside.

Marbles

How lucky am I? A ladder was suspended above my
head and as I stood up it jabbed my shoulders
leaving dual 1/4 inch squares where I can now store the
marbles that leak from my head.

Ursula Worm

Oh bloody fish gills! How will we explain this silk to the
Ursula worm? She holds the copyright and we didn't get
permission to spin!

W

Being a double you, he required twice the
space as his buddies and was often called upon
to "sit this one out."
He felt they were wordy, using two letters to his one,
and was all too pleased
to be set aside.

Discovery

Each morning, my eyes lunge toward the sun as if they'd
never been introduced. I know it's inappropriate to stare, yet
at this discovery, they can do nothing less.

Beneath Your Fur

I didn't mean to crop up beneath your fur this way –
your hair between my teeth is an addition I could
certainly have done without.

Wear It Not

I wear it not on my breast or heart bone. I let it drag at my
feet and fall away. It doesn't belong to me anymore.

Asylum

Do me a favor. Grant me asylum aboard your exquisite
feathered craft. I'll pack light of course, only a small
carry-on. And I'll even provide a map unless
you already know my direction.

Gratitude

She glanced up at the mitt and
unraveled its stitches with her smile.
In gratitude, it ensconced her feet
like moccasins.

Wonder Children

Plenty of young people point pencils at parallel
planes to their page. These wonder children
remain at the back of the class.

Let's Dance

Out in the sun she spat her glee,
at the foot of a petrified mulberry tree.
And for the first time in many years,
abated the tree's unrealistic fears.
No more tears – let's dance.

Roost

This is not so much a nest as a roost where I can lie
gingerly atop the twigs, taking flight at any given moment.
No roots around my soul, I am indeed free to indulge
the heights of this existence.

Golden Tears

Leave the crying to those who produce golden tears;
their sorrow is most beneficial.

Finland

There was no reason to fill space a certain way. I could
shape as I pleased, on the sofa or midgait across the rug —
fluid, uncontained, easy. It was the best of times.
Now Finland escapes me.

Will...

tree's leaves drip
morning dew over
the placid pond,
leaving divots
where raindrops
may gather undetected?

Will...

forests scream out in pain
every time another leaf turns red
and plummets to the ground?

Again it's morning.
How does that happen
day after day?
You'd think
after all this time
just once
morning would forget to appear.

✧

I continue
to walk
a fine line
between
repulsion
and passion.

✧

Because her punctuation was
always
a
step
behind,
she strolled without exclamation.

Should we forego our unctions
to propagate naturally and assume a
nondescript polymer instead?
What are we saying here?

✧

It needs to be interpreted.
Say it's an orange!
Let there be no doubt.

Nailed it to my centrifuge
alongside my dwellfurlotton.
Feels pretty good.

✧

Contemplative,
erratic,
peculiarly shaped...
she caught his eye.

Who trains the cow players to dance
so beautifully across the meadow?
Can anyone join their troupe?

✧

As much as I'd love to
pretty up the trees,
nature always beats me to it.

✧

Night fell.
And though no one was around to lift it up,
it carefully rose and walked away.

Accessorize the gull
with pearls and a gold boot;
it'll confuse the flock
and buy us more time.

✧

I startle easily once peace sets in.

To life in the new madras shirt.
May it never bleed.

✧

Remember me not,
for I've already forgotten you.

ULTIMATELY

The oddity of it all
emphasizes the need for it.

Afterword

I'm convinced I cultivated my sense of sharply ironic
humor as an embryo, somehow knowing I'd need it later on.

I began creating at age 8 by designing cardboard-sole shoes,
which eventually led to 12 years as a potter/sculptor,
13 years as a painter, and about 5 years now as a writer.
As a classically trained artist, I'm able to utilize a variety of
media, or do they use me? I wonder.

My propensity toward the misshapen, erratic side of life
is evident in most of my work, though I've painted my fair
share of notable realistic portraits. Following 9 years of
serious painting, I unexpectedly began to write. It was
liberating, to say the least. I could be loud, nonsensical,
and brutally honest without uttering a sound. Though
the words were meant to amuse and defuse only me, I was
encouraged to illustrate and share them with others.
I'm still amazed anyone else understands them, and even
more pleased that they're helpful.

I plan to continue my work through cards, books, paintings,
sculpture, whatever form it decides to take, because frankly
I'm unable to stop. I work in my Tucson, Arizona studio
which is attached to a tiny house containing
my husband and cat.